L❤VE LESSONS

FOR SINGLE **"HAPPY"** GIRLS AND THEIR NOT SO HAPPY FRIENDS

TERRÉ L. HOLMES

TURNER HOLMES
PUBLISHING HOUSE

ISBN 13: 978-0-9903275-0-9
Typesetting: Marion Designs
Editor: Stephanie Grair Ashford

Library of Congress Cataloging-in-Publication Data;
Turner Holmes Publishing House, LLC

Love Lessons by Térre L. Holmes
For complete Library of Congress Copyright info visit;
Turner Holmes Publishing House, LLC

Printed in U.S.A.

Dedication

This book is dedicated to all of the single happy and not so happy girls of the world. It is dedicated to those of you who choose to be single and to those who are single because it has chosen you. You are not alone and there is nothing *wrong* with you. In fact, you are imperfectly perfect, just the way you are.

It is also dedicated to the countless men and women who have knowingly and unknowingly shared their stories of love, commitment, and sacrifice with me over the years so that this book could have life. My experiences alone weren't enough to bring you the full depth of reality that one opens themselves up to in their quest for love and happiness. I am forever grateful to them all.

I would also like to dedicate this book to my father who has always made me feel loved. He never gave me a reason to doubt myself, but gave me a thousand reasons to believe in myself. Also, to my uncle Dennis, an exemplary husband, father, uncle, and friend; the man who stepped in and guided me in more ways than he will ever know and for that I am forever grateful.

Contents

Acknowledgement..VI

Introduction..VIII

He Won't Make You Happy......................................1

Believe Them...6

Stop Picking...15

Forgive Them..21

Be Free to Love...28

Know When All Bets Are Off.....................................37

Scratch Your List...45

Compromise...51

Numbers Matter..58

Cinderella Lost Her Shoe, Not Her Virginity..............65

Be Selfish...70

Education First..75

You're Going to Put Up With Something....................80

Get a Life...87

Love Thyself...93

Have It Your Way..101

You're Imperfectly Perfect.......................................109

Poetic Expressions of Love......................................115

Paradise...116

Before You..118

He is Love...120

The Morning After...122

That Kind of Love...123

In Conclusion..126

About the Author...130

Acknowledgements

I would like to thank my mother Brenda Holmes and my paternal and maternal grandmothers, Evelyn Turner and Lillie Jean Holmes as well as my aunts, Rhonda, Pam, and Kim. You have loaned me your shoulders to cry on and have helped shape me into the woman I have become through your love, support, personal sacrifice, and understanding. You are some of the strongest warrior women I know. Through nature I am strong and resilient; through nurture I am so much more.

I would also like to acknowledge my sisters, LaTasha, Marketta, and Nautica, and a host of amazing sister friends, including Kellie, Alice, Lisa Gibson, Nirvana, Mary, Cleatrice, Jamie, Marjorie, and Tara. All of you are some of the most amazing women I know, and I thank you for gracing me with your presence and blessing me with your love.

Thank you to the countless hands that edited, read, and reviewed this work over the years, Malika Ali, Mia Stokes, Harriet Bell, Moonyene Jackson, and Stephanie Grair Ashford who did the final edits. This work is far better than I could have ever imagined because of you.

Introduction

I know a thing or two about being single, but more importantly, I know the value of being happy and single. That is not to say that I haven't had my not so happy days as a single woman, but I've come to realize that being single is all about what you make of it. I don't necessarily wear it as a badge of honor, but I've accepted the fact that until I meet that special guy, I'll continue doing what is necessary to make *me* that special girl just for him.

    With that said, this book has been an evolution of sorts. It has challenged me to think about what's important to me as a single woman and the decisions I've made or didn't make in my own pursuit of love and happiness. I've learned a lot on this journey. So much so, that I felt compelled to put it into a book. I now know that being in a loving, fulfilling relationship does not happen by chance, but it happens through commitment: a commitment mostly to my *own* spiritual and emotional development.

Like many single 30-something women, I have a few relationships under my belt. I've also spent a great deal of time in conversations with singles and married couples. Likewise, I've paid extra close attention to my own behaviors and attitudes about long-term commitment. As a result, I found times when my views were skewed at best or even fanciful. I thought that a man was supposed to be everything *I* wanted him to be; I thought little of what I needed to be for *him*. I now know that these views didn't leave much room for a healthy relationship to flourish. However, through some prayer, a few therapy sessions, and a ton of self-help books, I finally began to make sense of my own psychosis, and this new found understanding couldn't have come any sooner.

I've learned that dating past 30 is different than dating in your 20's because in your 20's, your prospects seem endless. In your 20's, you can almost approach dating like a dinner buffet; there's so much to choose from that you don't know where to start. While in your 30's, your dating diet has changed. You don't like this and you can't stomach that; but honestly, there isn't as much to choose from. Consequently, you spend your time picking over the best of what's left over.

The harsh reality is that you might also be

the best of what's left over if you're in your mid to late 30's, but if you're 20-something, don't be in a mad rush to marry. On the other hand, don't overlook the good guy that might be a little on the short side, too nerdy or not so GQ. He just might turn out to be the not-so-perfect guy for you.

I'm here to tell you that the *perfect* guy simply doesn't exist. Truth is, we will all sacrifice something for love, whether it's height, good looks, personality, in-laws, finances, you name it. He won't come perfectly packaged, but the key is how *you* come packaged, not him. The key is in making sure that you're doing what it takes to be the best single happy girl you can be. Whether you marry or not, work on being a great woman for yourself and for those who love you in spite of your imperfections, your quirkiness, your bad manners, or whatever else you come packaged with.

Remember, you are the best example to other single girls, young and old of what singlehood can look like. Remember, there are other single girls looking up to you and gathering their examples from the single, happy life you live. So, be a good example. Be thankful for this solo time to live life on your own terms. Decide to be healthy, mentally, emotionally and spiritually, but most importantly, be happy for where you are, because when you're not happy for what you have, will you ever be happy when you have more? Being single is not always a choice, but being single and happy is.

LESSON 1
He Won't Make You Happy

I'm not happy being single, but I am happy. You might wonder how this could be. Well, I stopped being *unhappy* about my status years ago when I realized that being married wasn't a prerequisite for happiness, and all the married people I knew weren't exactly the happiest. However, I didn't come to that realization until well into my 30's. When I realized that my worth had nothing to do with whether or not I had a mate on my arm, but more about how I felt about Terré and the relationships I already had around me (which included supportive and loving family and friends), that was the turning point in my singlehood.

During those years of discontent, I recall thinking that if I had a man in my life to make me happy, everything would be perfect, but that was so far from the truth. The truth was that over the years I'd had several good men in my life, but I was *never* happy. For a long time I couldn't see that the real problem resided in me. I had not dealt with my childhood trauma and issues of neglect and abandonment from growing up in a family riddled with addiction. I didn't know this, but it was time that I stopped blaming my parents for what they did and didn't do. It was time to "woman up" and accept the fact that nothing in my life would change if I wasn't willing to change.

There were some words of advice offered to me by a guy I was dating some years ago. He shared with me something that his father had always said to him. He would say, "Son, it may not be your fault, but it is your problem." Sure, the things that had occurred in my life were out of my control and not my fault, but the facts were, those things had altered my world completely in a not so good way. I was filled with disdain and distrust for those who had given me life, and I was taking it out on everyone in my life, including myself. None of this was my fault, but now, as an adult, how I dealt with these *issues* was my problem and my problem only.

You may think that finding the *right* man will make you happy, but I'm here to tell you that it's a myth. It's actually more like a lie that we tell ourselves to cover up the real problem. Finding a man doesn't make you happy; it adds to your happiness *if* you're already happy. If you're not happy without him, chances are you won't be happy with him. A mate is to *add* to our lives not make our lives. Simply put, our lives are what *we* make them. No one should be responsible for making us happy, and who wants that responsibility when we won't even do what it takes to make ourselves happy?

So, are you happy, and if not, what would it take to make you happy? Have you accomplished the financial or career goals you've set for yourself? Have you lost the weight that you've been putting off? Do you have the kind of relationships that add to your happiness-- family and friends who support you and contribute positively to your life spiritually and emotionally? Have you made peace with the past? Only you know what will make you happy and if you don't, then it's time that you start to search deep within yourself to figure it out. You owe it to yourself to find your source of happiness, independent of a mate. After all, single girls really *can* be happy even if they'd prefer to be in a relationship, and single happy girls deserve and attract happy partners.

Reflections

What did this chapter cause you to reflect upon?

What are some of the things that make you the happiest outside of a relationship?

Identify a time in your life when you looked outside yourself to find happiness.

What was the result and how did it make you feel?

Are you happy with your station in life personally and/or professionally? If not, why not?

What would it take to make you happy personally and/or professionally? If you are happy talk about what it is that makes you happy personally and/or professionally.

LESSON 2
Believe Them

When I was 32, I met a man at the local bookstore who, as it turned out, lived on my street, just a few doors down. He was a great conversationalist, well traveled, mature, and extremely nice to me. In the beginning, he took me out to lavish restaurants on a regular basis; we shared similar visions for our lives and talked about everything from world politics to local arts and culture. I was caught up in his intelligence. His worldviews and profound wisdom fed me in a way that I had longed for my whole life.

It wasn't long before we were dating; yet our relationship was unsteady from the onset. I sensed that he was jealous, a little insecure, and perhaps, even a bit controlling, but I accepted it and even made excuses for it. After all, we were from two different cultures and had major differences in opinions about gender roles, family, and traditions.

It wasn't the end of the world, but it was enough to cause major friction in our worlds.

I was American and he Nigerian, and though we clashed in some areas, I was willing to overlook it all in my mad quest to "settle down". I was pleased that like me, he also believed in family and was ready to create one of his own. However, I had the feeling that it didn't have to be me because he was interested in whoever was willing and ready to take the leap. I just happened to be around at the time. He thought I was pretty, smart, and would make a good mother and wife (as he often told me), but I, on the other hand, wasn't so sure about him. It was all moving way too fast for me, but I never slowed it down. I simply thought that perhaps it was my time and who was I to question it?

Daniel was Nigerian and his aggressive nature often concerned me. One minute he could be extremely loving and kind towards me, but the moment he didn't like something that I had done or said, he was quick to blow up and spew out insults. I recall one particular evening, while we were in disagreement about something that really didn't matter at the end of the day, Daniel called me stupid. It was a shock to me, but even when I shared my anger over his insult, he never apologized. I didn't know it, but it was the beginning of the end for us.

I was offended for good reason and quickly told him so. No man had ever insulted me in that way, and I couldn't believe that it was happening at that moment. I left his house and refused to take his calls for days. That only intensified his efforts to get me back. He sent flowers, text messages, and left long voicemails, until I finally agreed to talk to him. I told him that his behavior was not acceptable and that under no circumstances was he allowed to talk to me that way again. I told him that I simply would not tolerate it in any relationship and if it happened again, it would be the end of us. He listened. He apologized. He vowed to never do it again. For the next 5 months he kept that promise.

One day Daniel and I got all dressed up for a fundraiser and joined my friends on a triple date in downtown Chicago at the W. It was a black tie affair and there were young, professional African-Americans everywhere. Daniel was a little older than most people in the room, and he didn't hang out with African-Americans on a regular basis outside of work. He would often share with me just how uncomfortable he was around the men in particular, but that's who my friends were.

Likewise, I wasn't accustomed to hanging out with Africans, but we both learned to make adjustments for the sake of our relationship.

We were all very excited to be attending the event and had been looking forward to it for a long time. One of my friends had traveled from Cleveland, so it was somewhat of a reunion for us as well. As the evening came to a close, we all decided to leave our cars with valet, grab a cab and continue our evening elsewhere. Daniel and the guys went to catch a taxi, but the lines outside of The W were extremely long as one could imagine, so the ladies notified the guys that we were dipping off to the washroom. We figured they could handle hailing a taxi without us.

We were gone for a matter of minutes when my cell phone began to ring. It was Daniel. Before I could get a word out, he yelled into the phone, "Where the fuck are you? The cab is here! Get out here now!" I could not believe what I was hearing. He had never spoken to me in *that* way and it had been five months since he had called me stupid, but I kept my cool. I calmly let him know that we were in the washroom and that we would be out in a minute, that is, before he hung up on me.

Daniel embarrassed me that day, and I could say that I never saw it coming, but I did.

Honestly, my agenda was my motivation. I wanted to be married. I wanted a mate that would take care of the bills and take me on lavish vacations, which he was already doing. I wanted to fulfill my agenda, but what was it going to cost me to do it with him and would it be worth it? I never stuck around long enough to find out. I could not allow my "agenda" to get in the way of the good common sense that my family instilled in me, nor could I ignore the fact that Daniel had issues with trust. He had a need to control and this situation was only going to escalate if I stayed any longer.

Years ago, I watched a woman on Oprah, who was once the epitome of beauty. She had clear mocha skin, a bright smile with beautiful teeth, a super star body, and a golden personality according to family and friends. She was a college graduate and the proud mother of one. Married to a man who was handsome and intelligent by most standards, she had what every girl *thought* she wanted. The picture appeared perfect on the outside, until the day her estranged husband walked into her place of work, doused her hair with gasoline and set her afire.

Her husband didn't choose *that* day to become violent. There were signs of his abusive nature throughout their courtship. She saw them early on and made a decision to ignore them. Her intuition whispered to her time and time again and she ignored it. Her intuition shouted at her and she muffled it, but the funny thing about intuition is that it never lies and intuition is the friendly sister of the inevitable. When you ignore intuition, the inevitable is bound to happen much sooner than later.

I once heard Maya Angelou say, "When someone shows you who they are the first time, believe them." The woman's estranged husband had shown her who he was many times over, but she wanted so desperately to believe otherwise. Besides, she loved him. He was the father of her child and he was supposed to love her. I've been there and her story could have easily been my story. Have *you* ever overlooked someone's ill behavior and brushed it off as just another bad day? I know I have and it could have cost me much more than a slight embarrassment. It could have easily cost me my life.

I believe there are instances that warrant us giving someone the benefit of the doubt, but after the second, third and fourth time, you can pretty much determine how the chapter is going to end. Daniel had shown me more than one time that he was belligerent and unpredictable in his behavior. I couldn't stick around to watch how that story would end.

When someone shows you who they are the first time, believe them. I'm not saying that people can't change, but abusive men and women don't usually change because of the person they're with. They change because of the person they lose. Don't make excuses for bad behavior. Don't accept less than what you deserve. If it doesn't feel right, it probably isn't right, at least not for you.

Ironically, Daniel used to tell me that his mother would say, "When you're dating, remember to keep both eyes wide open and when you say, 'I do', put your hand over the right." In other words, watch his behavior, watch his actions and be well aware of everything around you, but when you say, "I do" know that you've now accepted him, flaws and all, so place one hand over your right eye and be happy with the man you've married. The time to find out who your future mate really is does not come *after* your commitment before God, it comes before you make that commitment. Don't let the good sex, the handsome face, or the lavish gifts cloud your vision. Keep both eyes *and* ears wide open, and you'll be amazed at what you might find. The bottom line-- don't ignore the signs and take heed to the little whisper, before it becomes a deafening shout that even the dead can't ignore.

Reflections

What did this chapter cause you to reflect upon?

Identify a time when someone showed you exactly who they were, but you ignored the signs and it cost you in the end.

What did it cost you?

What could you have done to avoid the pitfall?

What did you learn in the end?

Why do you think most people ignore the signs?

LESSON 3
Stop Picking

Do you know this woman? She's the one with a laundry list of things that are wrong with the men she meets, but she has just as many flaws herself. He's too fat, but she's no supermodel. He doesn't have enough money, but she has more debt. He doesn't want children, but she doesn't like children. He has bad teeth, but she has bad breath. He lives with his parents, but she doesn't pay her rent on time. I mean, the list goes on and although everything she says about him is true, as the saying goes, "every time you point one finger at someone else, there are two fingers pointing back at you."

Honestly, I think that women are much pickier than men. I have a friend who explains it this way: "Men add and women subtract." When men meet women they don't start off saying that they've met someone and she's perfect. Men start somewhere in the middle and along the way they add to the list.

She can cook, check. She's good with my kids, check plus. She's a good listener, another check. Women on the other hand do the opposite. They tell their friends, he's amazing on Thursday and by Saturday she's telling her friends, how he didn't open the car door on their Friday date and how he didn't call to see if she made it home safely from the gym on Monday night. By the end of the following week, he's gone from amazing to being treated like a telemarketer and she's demanding he place her on the "do not call" list.

Ladies, we're not perfect and can I let you in on a little secret. I was that woman, until I realized that I was *that woman*. The one who found everything wrong with him and believed that his flaws were the reason why I was single. The truth of the matter was that if I'd never met him and his flaws, someone else would have come along with just as many issues to give me just as many reasons as to why I hadn't found the love of my life. And as my mother says, "Issues mean it's you!"

My advice is simple- stop trying to fix him and work on yourself. There are women with grocery lists of attributes that they desire in a mate and if they stacked their attributes up against his, they would see that they don't even measure up to their own ideal man! Many single women want men to be the very thing they are not, *perfect*. Do yourself a favor. Write out a list of 10 things you're looking for in a mate and then check off each one that coincides with who you are. For instance, you want him to be in good shape. Are you? You want him to be loving and giving. Is that you? Do you measure up to what you say you want? If the answer is no, then rethink your list *or* start doing what it takes to get *you* where you want him to be.

Guess what? Single women are no different than married women. I know plenty of women whose mission in life is to change their husbands. I don't know about you, but I don't like it when I feel like someone isn't accepting me for me. I get offended when someone is constantly harping on everything that's wrong with me, but not taking a minute to look in the mirror to see the imperfect image standing before them. In God's eyes we are all perfect. If only we had God's eyes.

I know a woman who is so fixated on how imperfect her fiancé is. Her claim is that he's irresponsible with his money, but yet, she's irresponsible with her words. For instance, she talks about how he doesn't do any work around the house. She complains about his poor choice in friends and how bad his credit is, and it's no secret to anyone that she makes more money and in her words, "his best asset". It's bad enough that she feels this way, but what's worse is that she'll share it with *anyone*. If you met her today, she'd say it to you!

I know she doesn't mean any harm, but harm is being done and my question is, could this be you? If so, whether you're in a relationship or not, you might want to stop staring so hard at his flaws, perhaps just long enough to see your own. In doing so, you might see some things that don't look so pretty with that new purse you just bought. You might see something in you that if you change it, that *one* change alone might help your mate become a better man. It's true! When we change, the people around us change too.

Whether you've chosen him *or* you're still waiting for him, whichever the case may be, your time is better spent working on you. You can't change people, and I'm a firm believer that people *make changes* out of their own desire to make others happy. If they desire to change they will, but if you're in a relationship, nagging them about everything won't get it done faster or make it go away. Work on you and as you do so, your mate may feel motivated to do the same. The late, great Mahatma Gandhi said, "Be the change you want to see in the world." If everyone in a relationship only focused on that, imagine how much happier people would be.

Reflections

What did this chapter cause you to reflect upon?

Identify a situation when someone "picked you apart". How did it make you feel? Did you tell the person? Why or why not?

Identify a time when you picked someone else apart. How did it make you feel?

How do you think it made them feel?

What benefits do people get from picking others apart?

LESSON 4
Forgive Them

I believe in the power of forgiveness, because it has changed my life. In fact, it gave me my life back. I didn't choose to forgive because it was the "right" thing to do; I learned to forgive because I needed to be free from the past. There's a quote, which says, "To forgive is to set a prisoner free and then to realize the prisoner was you." I was a prisoner for a very long time, stuck in the past and unable to see how it was affecting my present, and ultimately, my future.

The story began in 1974, when I entered the world amidst chaos. My parents were teenagers who had dropped out of high school, but met when they returned to pursue their high school diplomas. As well, they were like many young people in the 70's, looking for a way out from unemployment, limited opportunities, and ongoing segregation that still existed in many ways, in both the North and the South.

The 70's were challenging for many young African-Americans as drugs flooded their communities and lured them into its dangerous path. My father picked up a drug habit when he was around 15 and my mother eventually picked up one as well in her late 20's. My childhood was fraught with anger and unpredictability and my parent's choices as young teen-age parents would later cost me thousands of dollars in therapy and years of destructive and counter-productive behavior. In my late 20's, I started my quest in search of the healing that I hoped would set me free.

I found my healing through my work as a teacher and professional speaker, speaking on the power of letting go. Through this work, I was able to look at the past for what it was and for what it wasn't. The early years of my life left painful memories, childhood scars, and emotional trauma that would take me years to work through and as it stands, I am still a work in progress.

My journey towards forgiveness has been challenging at best, but I continue on this path because I know that not only does it free me, but it frees my relationships. I'm able to be in the moment with people and enjoy the gift of the present and leave the past in the past *if* I choose to. I still have challenges with forgiveness, but I understand how it affects my overall health and my relationships. I desire to not only be healthy physically, but to also be healthy mentally. Forgiveness is a huge piece to that puzzle.

Over time, I've learned that our love is connected to our forgiveness. Choosing not to forgive is like withholding love. I am not suggesting that you forgive the same accounts over and over again, but I am suggesting that when you do forgive that you leave it in the past and make a promise to yourself to stop revisiting it. It does our physical bodies no good and it is outright dangerous to the growth and development of our relationships.

I had to learn the hard way, that harbored resentment and bitter feelings for anyone doesn't end with just that person, but those feelings carry over into other areas of a persons' life *and* into other relationships. In fact, if a person has a hard time forgiving self or someone close to them like their parents, then they probably have a hard time forgiving most people.

If there is resentment from the past, let it go. Holding on to the past, not letting things go, and making others wrong so that you can be right are detrimental to the survival of *any* relationship. You may be thinking what does all of this have to do with *you?* The problems with forgiving can have a negative effect on *all* relationships, including your relationship with your children. Bottled up anger that you might be feeling towards someone else can easily and unknowingly be taken out on children. When negative emotions build up, we usually take it out on those closest to us.

Let it go, not just for yourself, but for any relationship that means anything to you. Let it go, because you want to experience better health and peace of mind. Let it go because it's going to free you up and allow you to get on with your life. And most importantly, let it go because single girls can't truly be happy if they're unforgiving. If you truly want to be a single happy girl, let it go because that's just what single happy girls do.

Think about your list. Every woman has one. It's her wish list for a mate. It's all the things she wants and thinks that she deserves. One of the things that I'm sure no one has on her list, however, is an unhappy man. Who would do that? So why do you think that you can be miserable by your own making and expect to have a mate that is the contrary? I'm not suggesting that you have to be perfect, because that's impossible, but I am suggesting that you work at the source of your unhappiness. Do what it takes to create your best self before you go adding someone else to your life expecting him to be something that you are not. As my good friend used to tell me, "Terre you're the CEO of your life", and I'm here to tell you that so are you! Ultimately, you are the one responsible for putting a smile on your face at the end of each day.

Reflections

What did this chapter cause you to reflect upon?

Do you find it more difficult to forgive yourself or others? Explain.

Recall a situation when someone didn't forgive you. How did it make you feel?

What do you think is the true cost of not forgiving others?

There is a quote that says, "When you forgive, you set a prisoner free and then realize that the prisoner was you." What does this quote mean to you?

LESSON 5
Be Free to Love

It's been said, "What you don't know can't hurt you." The truth is, what you don't know can *kill* you. Knowing your HIV status can mean the difference between life and death, so why is it that so many still don't care to know their status? We could blame ignorance, but with everything we now know about the disease and all of the advances in medicine, why remain ignorant? I think a word sums it up--fear.

Like many, I was afraid to know my status for years. I was highly promiscuous in my late teens and early 20's. I was afraid that if I got tested, with all of my caution-less escapades, I would certainly be positive. What were the chances that I could have unprotected sex on more occasions than I care to admit and escape the perils of the disease? Who was I to think that I was untouchable? Deep down I knew I was no different from the next person and *that* reality had me frozen in fear, unable to face the truth of the matter that I *might* be positive.

I finally gathered up the courage to be tested in 2000 while living in Brooklyn, New York. I can remember the day like it was yesterday. My current partner and I had just had unprotected sex when he leaned over to me, stared me in my face, smiled and said, "You've been tested right?"

In a panic, I blurted out, "Of course", and those words haunted me for days. I couldn't believe that I had lied to a man right in his face about my medical history. To make bad, worse, after he asked me that question, he rolled over and pulled his most recent status results from his wallet. He told me that he had been getting tested every year for the past 10 years! I was too embarrassed to tell him the truth, so I smiled, rolled over, and prayed to God that my lie wouldn't come back to haunt me.

The very next week I convinced a friend who had never been tested to go with me. Together we trotted into the Free Clinic in Brooklyn, left a little of ourselves behind, and then waited eagerly for a week to find out our fates. I don't know about her, but I was a nervous wreck! I couldn't eat. I couldn't sleep, and I couldn't imagine that with all I'd done in my life and who I'd done it with that

I'd escape unscathed. Thankfully, the old saying was proven true. God *does* take care of babies and fools. Though, at 26, I was no baby, I had surely exhibited some foolish behaviors.

For years to come, I remembered the man who changed my life just because he cared enough about his own to check his status. I thought that I never wanted to bring something like AIDS or any other diseases to a relationship, simply because I didn't care enough about my own health to check my status. It wasn't fair, and I vowed that every year, no matter what, I'd always get tested and always care enough about my fellow man to protect him if I could.

Fate would have it, while living in the Middle East back in 2010, I noticed a few bumps in my genital area. Not sure what they were, I visited the local OBGYN, only for him to tell me that I had genital warts and that if I didn't have them surgically removed immediately, they would get larger and leave scars on my skin. I was devastated by his prognosis and went into a depression for over a month, causing me to miss the last three weeks of work. How could this have happened to me? I wasn't having sex and had only had sex twice during the year that I was there.

I would later learn that most sexually active

people have genital warts and that the HPV virus that causes genital warts can lie dormant in individuals for years. I also learned that you can catch the HPV virus which causes genital warts with or without a condom. Once treated, it could take months or even years for the warts to actually disappear, but they sometimes come back. I was terrified of the news and feeling like I was absolutely too far away from home for something like this to be happening. I was in real deep stuff because in the UAE, it was illegal to have sex without being married. If they found out, my partner and I could be thrown in jail. Additionally, if it was discovered that I had a sexually transmitted disease, that was grounds for being arrested as well, because they would automatically assume that I had been sexually active while living in their country. My shady Iraqi doctor assured me that he would tell the hospital that I had caught my warts from a toilet seat. I had to pay him in cash to perform the surgery because if he reported it through my insurance company, I could be "found out".

Reluctantly, I agreed to surgery and paid him a down payment. I was a mess! How could this be happening to me and what did this mean for my future? I was already 37 and it was ill advised for a woman to have a child with genital warts, as she could pass them on to her unborn child. All I kept thinking was "why me and why now"?

In 6 weeks I was scheduled to go on a solo vacation to South Africa. I could go and then wait until I got home to the states to have a second opinion *or* I could let some foreign, scissor-happy doctor cut me up and risk the possibility of leaving that hospital without a clitoris! I had heard horror stories about doctors in the UAE. My Emirati colleague had said that she believed that all of the doctors who couldn't find jobs elsewhere flocked eagerly to the UAE for employment. After hearing and reading other horror stories about local doctors, I don't believe she was too far off!

I couldn't take any chances, so I cancelled my surgery and my trip to South Africa. I knew that if I went, I wouldn't enjoy myself, and I didn't want that to be what I remembered most about my trip. I decided to go home to the US for a second opinion, and I thank God everyday that I did. As it turned out, the bumps weren't genital warts after all. One was something called Molluscum Contagiosum, a viral disease which is contagious but is most seen in children on their arms and legs. It can also be transferred through sexual skin-to- skin contact or by touching something that has been touched by a contagious person. The other bumps, believe it or not, were hair bumps! You heard me. Hair bumps! I had gotten them because a month before, I had gotten a Brazilian Wax and they had popped up just after the Molluscum had appeared making me think that they were all related.

Back home in the US, the Molluscum was treated and immediately disappeared and the hair bumps went away, as hair bumps always do. I learned a heck of a lot from this ordeal. There was so much I didn't know about genital warts and Molluscum. Now, I'm even more cautious than I previously was. I value my body even more, and I realize that you can never be too careful. All of this was embarrassing, but even more so, it was eye-opening. More people are walking around with diseases they can't pronounce and knowingly or unknowingly passing them around. I don't want to be one of those people.

Single happy girls take care of themselves first. By taking care of themselves, those around them are protected as well. Keeping yourself and your partner protected, as well as getting tested, sharing your statuses, and choosing to be in a monogamous relationship, are steps responsible adults take, and if you're carrying around a disease that is transmittable through sexual activity, it's your obligation to let the other person know.

Single happy girls also don't blame the other person for getting "burnt", when they know that they didn't do everything they needed to do to protect themselves in the first place. If you're in a relationship and get burnt, that's one thing, but when you're freely having unprotected sex with someone you're not committed to and they're not committed to you, it's like having sex with strangers. Every time the two of you have sex, you're also having sex with all of their sexual partners as well as their partners' partners.

Being single takes work. It takes responsibility and it takes a lot of courage. Get yourself tested. Have the tough conversations with your partner and don't be afraid to say what you want and what you expect. I'm a lot smarter since my year in the desert, but I'm also a lot more cautious. I don't want to be another statistic, and I don't want to make someone else a statistic either. I want to love freely, have the right to choose whom I love, but I also want to be responsible for how I love. It's the only way to truly be single, happy and free.

Reflections

What did this chapter cause you to reflect upon?

In your opinion, what does it mean to love freely?

Is there a price we pay for loving freely? If so, what? If not, why not?

LESSON 6
Know When All Bets Are Off

Do you know what your deal breakers are? Not some unrealistic list concocted out of your girlhood fantasies, but real deal breakers that are significant and realistic? We all have them. What are yours? Which ones should you keep? Which ones need to be attached to a spaceship and launched out into space? I figured mine out through much trial and error and as I *grew up* or *grew older*, they changed. The longer you remain single, you will see yours do the same.

You see, what I wanted or thought I needed at 25, was not the case at 35. What was easy to find at 26 wasn't so easy at 36. For instance, at 26, there was a higher probability that if I chose to date someone my age, and I wanted him to be childless, never married, with a promising career, in great shape with *all* of his hair, I would have many candidates from which to choose. At 36, things looked a lot different. A greater number of those same men had children, ex-wives, child support, alimony and receding hairlines. So, what's a girl to do? I had to scratch a few things off my list, make some adjustments and stop looking for the boy I would have dated at 26, when the man I needed was staring me right in my face.

My deal breakers were plentiful, because I believed that the man I was in search of really did exist. Each time I broke up with one guy, I added a new deal breaker to my list. Boy, was I aimlessly traveling in circles! No man could measure up to what I considered my deal breakers. Furthermore, the list was too long to begin with. My original list had at least 25 things on it and it included the following:

He should be financially independent or practically rich. (What was I thinking?)
A great lover
Childless
Never Married
My family should love him
He should love my family
Well-educated
A great communicator
Patient

Kind
Get along well with my friends
He should be taller than me, not too skinny, but not too fat
He should have a very nice car and house and on and on and on

I should have stopped at numbers five and six, because, truly, my folks aren't the easiest people to get along with. What I didn't realize was that my list was digging me deeper and deeper into a hole that I couldn't get myself out of. If I dated according to my *list* I would have been a very lonely woman in Chicago, so I adjusted the list, became more realistic and learned to be more appreciative of different types of men. That has served me well.

So again, what are your deal breakers? In a relationship, deal breakers are those things that you simply can't live with or without. In fact, most people's top deal breakers tend to be universal like mental and physical abuse, drug addiction and infidelity. Those are the deal breakers that most of us would choose to live without. However, we enter some gray areas when we start to talk about preferences. Of course, the list of deal breakers varies for everyone. What one woman prefers may not be as important for another. One thing for certain is that I must have an intelligent man, someone who stimulates me mentally. In fact, I'm willing to take brains over beauty, as well as brains over extreme wealth. Money isn't as important to me as intellect, but that's just my preference. Everyone is different and the key is making sure that your deal breakers are logical and reasonable and not just an excuse for you to be ultra picky, because no one is going to come packaged exactly as we want and happy single girls know this to be true.

Single happy girls also know that no one is perfect. Our grandparents may have told us we were perfect in an effort to make us feel better as a child, but as adults, we now know differently. Perfection is only found in fairytales and even then, Cinderella would probably have not been looked at twice if she hadn't been all dolled up for the ball. None of us are perfect and we shouldn't expect our mates to be either. Let's face reality, the reason why we all got excited as children when we entered a candy or toy store was because there was so much to choose from. Without choice and variety, what a dull world this would be.

Below is a list of deal breakers. They are not etched in stone, but they simply are a compilation of what a sample of 50 women from different walks of life, ethnicities and religious backgrounds found to be important to them. It is derived from many personal conversations I have had with women around the world. You may find that some of these work for you while others don't. It's perfectly fine; take what you like and toss the rest. Just know what it is that matters to you and once that becomes clear, I'm a firm believer that when you know what you want, you won't waste time on what you don't want. Here are a few deal breakers I've gathered over the years:

He must love children
He must not be physically/emotionally abusive
He must believe in a power higher than himself
He must be drug and addiction free
He must be employed and ambitious
He must be polite to others, including family and friends
He must be giving and loving
He must be a good communicator
He must be trustworthy and honest
He must be financially responsible
He must have a healthy self-image and self-esteem
He must be affectionate

If these deal breakers work for you, that's great! If not, find what works for you, keep it, and toss the rest. There is nothing wrong with having a set of criteria for dating. Know what matters to you, so that when you see it, you recognize it and you can embrace it as such. It also helps you create a standard to live by and sets the stage for what is to come in your relationships.

Reflections

What did this chapter cause you to reflect upon?

Do you think that it's important for everyone to have deal breakers? Why or why not?

List your five top deal breakers. Be fair, be honest, but above all, be real with yourself.

They say that in relationships, everyone settles for something. If this is true, do you believe that settling is a bad thing? Why or why not?

- Must know God and have an open relationship (authentic)
- must be an excellent communicator
- Must be patient and affectionate
- Must believe in improving himself mentally, physically and sexually

LESSON 7
Scratch Your List

Now that you've made your list, scratch it! That's right. If you're the girl looking for *thee* guy, I have one piece of advice- scratch that list! I mean, stop limiting yourself. You don't know whom you're missing out on because of your *list*. As an African-American woman, I realize most African-American women will never be married, because they are way too limited in their thinking when it comes to finding a mate. I experienced this growing up in my hometown of Cleveland, Ohio, on the east side, where it's a rare occasion to see an African-American woman with a non-black man. It's just not something that African-American women do in Cleveland.

Many African-American women almost believe that it is a betrayal to marry outside of the race. Furthermore, many of them don't find white men attractive or macho enough or they're too afraid to talk to them because of the racial divide that exists in America. As America becomes more and more of a melting pot, we must learn to work through those limitations and begin to see people for people and not the color of their skin. However, if you're stuck on "color", heed an insight a male friend shared with me. "There are several continents for black women to choose from where black men (or me of color) exist." Must he be a black man or white man or whatever else you've decided in your mind? Why can't he just be a man who loves you for you?

When we start limiting our romantic prospects based on ethnicity, we further decrease our chances of finding love and I'm not just speaking to African-American women. This conversation is for women of all ethnic origins, because we all suffer from a disease of sameness. If it doesn't look like anything we're accustomed too, then we don't want to try it. The truth of the matter is just because someone looks like you (or me) or comes from where you come from, doesn't mean that you two have much else in common. If you opened yourself up, you might be shocked to find that you actually have more in common with the person who looks nothing like you and who originates from the opposite side of the world.

Ladies, get outside of your boxes and do away with your self-imposed limitations. If you'll only date one type of man, think about all of the men you're missing out on in the world. The world is way too diverse to put limitations on what is possible. Besides, no one really knows where one will find love or how it will come packaged. That's why it's imperative that you remain open. Your Mr. Romeo could be sitting next to you on your next flight to West Africa or the guy you pass every day at the water cooler who smiles at you but is just a little afraid to speak up. If you have the personality for starting conversations, don't write him off, spark up a conversation and see where that leads you. You never know. He might not be the one, but he might be the one who leads you to the one.

As single happy girls, it's important that we see opportunity in all things, but it's difficult to see it when we're limiting ourselves. We mustn't limit ourselves in any area of our lives and we must know that in order to find the love we want, we have to put ourselves in the path of that love. For instance, if you work from home and never go into an office, you should find other opportunities to interact with people, whether it's joining a social group or taking a class or even starting up a venture of your own. As well, if you work and that's all you do, then maybe you should consider an outing after work every once in while. That could mean seeing a movie or play with a coworker or meeting some friends out for dinner. The more you put yourself out there, the more you increase your chances. Once you're out there, you have to also be friendly. Talk to people and be receptive to meeting strangers. I know this might seem painful for some, but as they say in the gym, "no pain, no gain." Besides, anything is possible if you're willing to give it a try and nothing's possible if you're not.

Reflections

What did this chapter cause you to reflect upon?

What are the top five attributes that you MUST have in a mate?

LESSON 8
Compromise

Have you considered what you can live with *and* what you simply can't live without? Perhaps you've made a list. Or, maybe that list is buried somewhere deep within your subconscious. Whatever the case may be, in relationships this is a very important question to ask yourself. Each of us owes it to ourself and our relationship to consider those things which we know we can live with and determine what those things are that we simply can't live without.

Now, understand this. When you finally say, "I do", there may be some things that you thought you couldn't live without, that you end up compromising on. The key is, once you say, "I do" and you discover there's that one thing that didn't quite make the cut, stop longing for it. Become content with living without it and I guarantee you, your life and your relationship will be much better off. There is nothing worse than longing for something in your marriage or mate that you know is never going to come to fruition.

For example, instead of being tall, dark, and handsome, he's short, stout and fair. No matter how much you wish for something else, he couldn't change even if he wanted to. I know that may sound silly, but sometimes we fall in love with people who may be missing a few things that we put on our *must have* list.

Once you say, "I do", give it up, let it go, and be happy, because if you don't, you will find yourself longing for something that does not or can not exist. I don't know what that is for you. It's different for everyone. Some people are secretly wishing that they had married someone who makes more money. Well, if that's you, give it up! You didn't. Therefore, instead of complaining or longing for it, choose to be happy with what you have. However, there's also nothing wrong with motivating your current mate to reach greater career and financial heights *if* that is what he also wants for himself, and you're not doing it in a nagging way. There will be benefits for the both of you.

On the other hand, if you know that your

mate has reached his limit or that he may not have it in him to make the type of money to match the lifestyle you desire, you have two choices-- make the money yourself or accept the man you married for who he is. Don't try to change him because I assure you, there was probably something on his "must have" list that he wrote off to be with you.

If what you're longing for is greater than material worth or possessions, for instance, if your "must have" was to have a mate that is affectionate and considerate and you still desire that, then by all means, talk with your mate about it. If necessary, suggest that the two of you seek counseling or attend intimacy workshops together. Perhaps there's a book worth reading together like Gary Chapman's *The Five Love Languages*. It's not always a matter of throwing out the baby with the bath water.

There are no guarantees that any of this will work, but it's worth a try. Besides, when there is any type of void in physical and emotional intimacy, our natural instinct is to fill that void. If the problem really is you and no matter what your mate does to please you, you're still not happy, then either get the help *you* need to work on yourself or just accept him as he is and understand that this may be one of those things that you must live without. It is much easier to live without one thing when the list of positive traits are so very vast, than it is to complain about the one or two things you don't like and risk losing a man who had 90% of what you view as important.

If you feel depleted in multiple areas that were on your "can't live without" list, then maybe you should start reevaluating who you married and why. You just might find that the problem really lies in you and your desire to be in a relationship clouded your judgment in choosing a mate. At the end of the day, the bottom line is not to be longing for things that we can't have. Looking to the past for what didn't happen or what you didn't get is like trying to drive while watching the rearview mirror. You can't get ahead in any area of your life, if you're always focused on what's behind you. An ancient African proverb says, "Start with what you have, from where you are, right now" and consider these three questions.

What's your mental state right now?
What are you unhappy with as it pertains to your relationship?
What can you do to make what you have, work for you, right now?

The bottom line is, don't lose a sure thing, for a maybe and don't let some one else's grass cloud your view of your own. What you might be seeing over their fence is synthetic turf, when you've got the real thing at home. With a little cultivation, nurturing and love, it could be just as beautiful as what you *think* your neighbor has.

Reflections

What did this chapter cause you to reflect upon?

When you hear the word "compromise" what does it make you think of?

What are some of the areas you are not willing to compromise in? Explain.

Identify one area that someone may have to compromise in, in order to be with you and is it fair to ask him or her to do so?

LESSON 9
Numbers Matter

Believe it or not, debt to income ratio, FICO scores, and credit worthiness are actually just as important as what kind of car a guy drives and equally as important as whether or not he has a J-O-B or can make your toes curl! Yes, the latter is very important, but the former can kill the future of any match made in heaven. Why? Because how your future mate manages or mismanages money is critical to both of your financial futures. And if your mate is in financial ruin, it's imperative that you find out sooner than later.

I know money is scary to talk about, but it is a topic that far too many people ignore and end up very disappointed once they realize they've signed their name on the dotted line of someone else's mound of debt. Some people make the mistake of talking about it too prematurely, judging their mate, before they've gotten an opportunity to know them. Everyone isn't a "dead beat" when it comes to paying their bills and paying them on time. Some people really have hit rock bottom for one reason or another and have used credit to bail themselves out, whether it's the loss of a job, a divorce, an illness, or a business deal gone awry; it can happen to any of us.

However, when the time is right and only you know when that is (maybe a year into the relationship *or* when you sense that the two of you are considering merging households or actually getting engaged), find out what you're getting yourself into. Once you say, "I do", you can no longer say, "his debt" or "my debt". It is now, "our debt". Not knowing the magnitude of your mate's debt in detail is like walking into a gunfight with a bat!

You have to know what you're dealing with before you walk into the situation or you'll feel unprepared or worst yet, unmotivated to deal with the situation at all. You need to be honest about your finances as well and once you both are on the same page, sit down and come up with a game plan to get you through. This is an extremely important chapter, because one of the major causes of divorce is attributed to financial problems. Talk about the money, plan to resolve any issues and seek counseling if necessary, but don't become a statistic if you don't have to.

Statistics show that the number one killer of relationships is money. We are a society consumed by debt. We have everything we need and most of the things we want, and we're still not happy. So what do we do? We go out and acquire more. Ask yourself this question, if you got married today and your mate unfortunately died 6 months later, leaving you with debt that he accumulated long before he met you, would it be fair for you to be responsible for clearing up that debt, even though you didn't help to create it? I'm sure your answer is, "absolutely not", but, once you say, "I do", you're not just saying, "I do" to the relationship, you're also saying, "I do" to your mate's prior financial responsibilities.

A healthy relationship should start out with a healthy perspective on money and debt. You don't want to enter into a lifelong union and find that it's more of a liability than an asset. No one wants to feel like they can't get ahead because of unwise decisions made by someone else, nor should anyone want to be a financial burden to their future mate. Start off on the right foot. Work to do everything within your power to clear up debt and to keep it away, whether it's your debt or his. There will be enough things that warrant your attention in this union. Unnecessary debt shouldn't be one of them.

Besides, when you have an extraordinary amount of debt looming overhead, your actions are dictated by your need for money and not your real pursuit and passion to experience and enjoy life. I once read a quote that said, "You should work to live, not live to work." When you can't afford to do the things that you are truly passionate about, when there is no discretionary income to travel or to get out and spend quality time together, life can become real mundane. When life feels that way, look at all of the unnecessary pressure that's being put on your union.

Know that everything we need, we already have and everything we want we don't need. That simple lesson will lead you to evaluate what's important to you and if looking like a million bucks is more important than actually accumulating a million bucks through hard work and sacrifice, then I'm not speaking to you. Life is about choices. The choice you make to spend without a budget, to buy everything you think you need and to accumulate more debt than necessary is a choice that you unfortunately are making alone, but you can also make a choice not to force someone else to live under the same stress that you have subjected yourself to day in and day out.

The last thing you want is to have your mate say is "I can't afford to marry you." Let's face it, most of us aren't meeting and marrying wealthy ballplayers and businessmen, and even if you were, who in their right mind would invest in a depreciating asset? When you are in debt over your head, each and every day you are losing value emotionally and spiritually. Who can live a whole and healthy life robbing Peter to pay Paul? Bottom line is this- seek to become whatever it is you desire in a mate financially. If you want him to be responsible with his income and resources, seek to become that which you desire in him. It's only fair that if he comes to the table with a sound financial future, so should you or at least be willing to work on it.

Reflections

What did this chapter cause you to reflect upon?

Do you think that credit and debit cards can control a relationship? If so, how?

Have you ever been in a relationship that was "ruled" by money, either the lack of it or use of it to control someone else? How did it make you feel?

Is money enough to make you stay in a relationship and is the lack of money enough to make you leave? Explain.

LESSON 10
Cinderella Lost Her Shoe, Not Her Virginity

Now that I have your attention, I read that headline on Twitter one day. It was written by one of my male followers. The Tweet went on to say, 'you don't need to have sex to find your prince'. I understand I'm talking to adult women and I'm telling you what to do with your vajayjay's (a term Oprah often uses), but if at least one of you was anything like me as a teen growing up, even though momma told me, "Don't go looking for love in all the wrong places" because she didn't know how to say, "Your stuff is golden and only meant for the man who understands that," then I'm talking to you too!

I'll admit, I didn't GET that lesson until well into my early 30's. Sadly, there are still many single 20-something and 30-something women who still don't get it. Your loving really is golden. Most men I know who are married, talk about how their wives made them wait, how they were friends first, as he watched her from afar or how he was just at that point in HIS evolution that sex wasn't *thee* most important thing and in the process, he found the woman he would marry.

No man wants easy, and I'll admit I've had to learn that the hard way. Although mom told me this, I didn't have the confidence in myself to believe it. In college, my cousin and I used to joke about girls giving sex away for a Happy Meal. This is not to say that sex is for sale, but my God we knew way back then that we deserved so much more. I don't know about you, but I've had an experience or two that left me asking, "What the heck did I do that for?" I won't go into details, because I'm a lady and ladies don't kiss and tell. However, I've kissed a few frogs because I didn't want to listen to momma, and boy, it was nothing to write home about.

The lesson is, there are still grown men telling women that they're not going to wait until she's comfortable to have sex because "we're all adults here and besides, I'm a man and I have needs." While I don't think we need Steve Harvey to tell us what we already know instinctively, I'm here to tell you, if it don't feel right, it ain't right! If you wait, at least 90 days as he suggested before giving up the goods, you will probably find that you're not really that interested in him to begin with and vice versa. If you're totally beyond this, I'm happy for you, but share it with a young woman who is still struggling. Tell her to find someone that will take the time to get to know her for all of who she is and not just for her fancy legwork beneath the sheets. I have found that special someone for myself and our journey has been one to write home about.

Reflections

What did this chapter cause you to reflect upon?

Do you think that sex is a mental, physical or emotional act? Explain.

How important is it to wait at least 90 days before having sex with a new partner?

Do you think that having sex too soon can have a negative impact on a potential relationship? Explain.

LESSON 11
Be Selfish

Happy single girls are selfish girls, and who says that there's anything wrong with being concerned with the needs of oneself? Putting self first is a sure fire way to be of better service to others. After all, if you don't have what you need, it makes it difficult to give others what they need. Unfortunately, we live in a society that tells us that being selfish is a bad thing and that selflessness is noble. I couldn't disagree more.

While it is nice to be noble, I know way too many women who are mentally, physically, and emotionally depleted because they've given others more than they've given themselves, and they regret it. I have met countless single and married women who regret not living more and doing more for themselves. While many of them have the chance to turn things around, there are many others who will never get that time back to go off to school, live abroad, buy nice things for themselves without feeling guilty about it, or just sit on the porch, read a book and do nothing all day.

As a married woman, should you walk down that path someday, there will be plenty of opportunities to be absolutely selfless, but as a single girl, learn to be good to yourself now. Pamper yourself, talk sweet to yourself and do the things that bring you joy because when you marry and start a family, it will be difficult to do those things when you're worried about making lunches, getting children to football practice and being there for the husband. The more practice you get with being good to yourself as a single girl, the more you get to use it when you're juggling between the happiness of others and yourself.

It's respectable, yet unfortunate that so many single moms put their child's needs above their own. However, I would encourage every mother to seek the balance between loving your child and loving yourself. That means, get your rest when you can, take care of your mind and body by exercising and eating properly, and take a break when you need it. If that means bartering with another mom, then make it happen. There are other single moms who need breaks and by forming a collective with them, you can barter babysitting services with one another from time to time or even pool your money together for a sitter on any given night.

Be creative if need be, but at all cost, be selfish sometimes. If you don't get the time, rest, or whatever else you require, stress and burnout will creep in and before you know it, you'll be suffering from depression and/or all sorts of diseases and ailments directly related to your lack of self-care.

You only get one you and no one is going to treat you better than you can treat yourself. After all, no one knows what you think, feel and need quite like you do. Listen to yourself. Don't tune yourself out. When you're tired, instead of trying to please the crowd by going out to dinner or catching that movie, decline. Take some time out for you, listen to your body and remember that you're the most important person in your world and you know best. If you're not happy, no one's happy.

Reflections

What did this chapter cause you to reflect upon?

What are some things you do when you need quality time alone?
What are some things you'd like to do more of?

What are some things standing in the way of you not getting the time you need for yourself?

What immediate adjustments can you make in your life, so that you can get the time you need to be good to yourself?

LESSON 12
Education First

I often meet women who are mothers of happy and healthy children. They have meaningful relationships with their mates. Sometimes they even find great joy in what they do professionally, but when I speak with them intimately about their hopes and dreams for their lives, the story is always the same. With all they have and all they've accomplished personally and sometimes professionally, there is still that one thing missing. Either they never completed their education, or they never went back to advance their education. Now they feel stuck.

Unfortunately, once many of us settle down and get married, it becomes increasingly difficult to focus our energy on being a good student, as well as an attentive wife and mother. It's not impossible, but it's much easier to get the degree out of the way when you are single and living your life for you and only you.

I am reminded of one of my girlfriends who got pregnant during our freshman year of college. She was forced to drop out of school for a short period of time, but with the help of her mother she was able to return a year later, only to get pregnant, again, during her junior year. She finally graduated after nearly six years, but she probably couldn't have done it without her mother's support.

Everyone isn't as blessed as she was to have a mother who stepped in and raised the children for her while she pursued her Bachelor's degree. Even after she graduated from undergraduate her mom stepped to the plate again and took care of her children when she moved out of state to work on her Master's degree. I am happy to report that she now has her education out of the way and is happily married, but it wasn't easy for her or the rest of her family. Together they managed to pull it off.

Sometimes, we need to focus on what's important today. If we are fortunate, tomorrow will come, but being prepared for tomorrow is a challenge we all must face. If advanced education is in your future, don't put it off. While you're single and have that free time on your hands, go for it! The day will soon come when life will become more about the needs of others and going back to school may become more of a distant desire. Why put off for tomorrow what you could do today? There is no day like the present and life is too short to live with regrets, wondering "what if?"

Reflections

What did this chapter cause you to reflect upon?

Do you believe it's important for a woman to have her education before she marries? Why or why not?

LESSON 13
You're Going to Put Up With Something

I know I told you to identify what your deal breakers are, and I want you to keep them because they're your internal guide for the type of relationship and person you want in your life. However, and this is a *BIG* however, you're going to have to learn to put up with *something* or you'll be single for the rest of your life. The fact is, everyone puts up with something, whether you know it or not. Our grandmothers dealt with certain behavior from our grandfathers. Our mothers tolerated certain behaviors from our fathers and your girlfriends tolerate certain behavior from their mates and spouses as well, but you don't have to believe me, ask them for yourself.

I don't know about you, but I always had a no BS policy in place. I didn't leave much room for negotiation and it was Terré's way or no way or some might say, 'Terre's way or the highway'. That was me and the more I thought about it, I realized, I was looking for the *perfect* guy and he was never going to show up on my doorstep because he simply didn't exist.

It took me a long time, to look around me and realize that all of my friends, cousins, aunts and anyone else I knew that was married or in long-term relationships hadn't chosen perfect mates. They had simply chosen that someone who they felt was good for them at the time, and they had decided to accept them just as they were. Those who couldn't accept their mates for who, and what they were, present company included... well... they ended up single.

I'm not suggesting that we single girls lower our standards. No, not at all. In fact, keep your standards high, but know that he will not come packaged perfectly and that you might have to "put up with something". I'm not sure what that *something* is. Maybe, he's cocky or too shy. Maybe he's a bit of a homebody, but he's a lot of fun to be around. Perhaps he's a little too silly for your liking, but on a positive note, he balances you. All I'm saying is that you can't have it all, and here's the big secret that everyone has been hiding from you-- *nobody does*.

Once you get over believing that you can be in a relationship and not ever put up with anything, the sooner you'll be on your way to experiencing a healthier relationship. I say healthy, because I didn't realize that my picking apart was unhealthy. My believing that I didn't have to tolerate *anything* was simply untrue. Bill and Hillary may look like the perfect couple, but Hillary suffered public humiliation when Bill had an affair with an intern in the White House. We all remember those famous words: "I didn't have sex with that woman Monica Lewinsky."

Don't misunderstand me, what Hillary put up with was trying for any woman, but I suppose she weighed the good and the bad and realized that there was more to love about Bill than there was to throw away. She had to make that decision for herself, just as we have to determine if we'll put up with the guy who may be a bit of a momma's boy, but yet he treats you just as good as he treats his mom. There are pros and cons to everything, and if your argument always leans towards what's lacking you'll never find a man good enough for you.

People often ask me why I am still single, and for a long time I couldn't answer that question. I didn't know that I was single by my own choosing. I had met great men who had the core qualities and values that any *smart* woman would jump on. Many of those men I met and dated along the way found other women who loved them and accepted those things that I deemed unacceptable. They are now married!

What I've come to realize is that everyone puts up with something. I'm sure that even Princess Diana put up with something to be part of the royal family. She undoubtedly faced some of the same issues that families around the world experience. Sad to say, even the life of a (real) princess isn't picture perfect.

Call it what you want. Some people may think that this realization came as a result of getting older and being single, and I'll tell them that they're absolutely right, but not for the reasons they believe. What's true about this train of thought is that as a result of getting older, I grew up. I matured and realized that I was living life in a fantasy world. I had honestly believed that I was going to find someone who fit all the criteria on my list. It was foolish and immature on my part, but I didn't know what I didn't know, and that one fact kept me single.

Here's my new formula. I ask myself what are his quirks and after I identify them, I ask myself if I could learn to live with them for a lifetime. If the answer is yes, then I'm willing to give him a chance, because after all, I most certainly have a few quirks of my own that he'll have to accept. I am imperfectly perfect for someone and there's someone out there who's imperfectly perfect for me.

Reflections

What did this chapter cause you to reflect upon?

What are some of your quirks that could stand to work on in your current relationship? *Or,* do you have a quark that has affected previous relationships?

What has it cost you? Is it worth holding on to? Why or why not?

LESSON 14
Get a Life

Lesson 14. Get a life. Find something to do that matters to you, other than work. Volunteering, exploring a hobby, traveling, or spending more time with loved ones are great places to start. Getting a life will do more for you than you could ever imagine; it will also work wonders for your relationship.

One of the most significant things to consider about getting a life is that it will help you keep your mind off the fact that you're single. It will also give you more to talk about, not in the braggadocios way, but more to offer in the way of a conversation and life experiences when Mr. Right finally does come along.

In my dating life, I have found that dating was a lot more fun when I had something else going on in my life. On the flip side, when I was going to work every day, coming home and waiting for *him* to call, life was real humdrum and so were my relationships. Life is a summation of experiences, both good and bad. If all you have to talk about is your day at the job, things can become really dull very quickly. Communication is important in a relationship and when you have a life, you're able to offer more to the conversation. When every day is the same, your mate can just about guess what to expect, and when he's able to predict your every move, that can be pretty boring.

However, getting a life is not just about the man in your life. It's about you. When you have something worthwhile going on, you just feel better. We were not made to just work. We were created to live, to experience this wonderful thing called life and then to share those experiences with others. In essence, we are a sum total of our experiences and when those experiences are lacking there can be a bit of a void on the inside.

I spent a year teaching in the Middle East. I worked with women who wore thousand dollar abayas, drove luxury vehicles, wore enough expensive jewelry to buy a house in an average US suburban community and got paid nearly triple what most of us Western teachers were making for the same job. However, the major difference between all of us was that the Emirati teachers were miserable. Many of them had not chosen teaching as a profession; it was chosen for them by their fathers or husbands. None of them had hobbies, spent any real time with anyone other than their families or got to decide much of anything for their lives. Their lives were not their own; therefore, the idea of *getting a life* wasn't even an option. They seemingly had everything and nothing, all at the same time.

So, what's exciting in your world? Do you belong to your church choir? Do you volunteer at the local food bank? Are you passionate about a certain cause? Who are you and why should he care to know you? Far too often we sit around waiting for life to happen once we have a mate. We tell ourselves that we'll start traveling once we meet him. We'll explore a particular hobby once he comes along. We put our lives on hold and then we wake up one day realizing that life has passed us by.

Life is happening right now, every day, right before our very eyes. Are you an active participant, or are you sitting on the sidelines watching someone else's life? The choice is yours. My sisters in Abu Dhabi didn't have any choice. Most of the decisions for their lives had been made for them, but that's not your story. Although you may feel like your life lacks luster just like them, you can do something about it! Explore a hobby. Dust off your passport. Take a class just for fun or just start spending more time with the people who matter. Not only will you add value to your life, but you'll add value to your other relationships. Getting a life will help you grow and will, in turn, help your relationships to prosper and grow. If you don't believe me, try it and watch from the inside, how your life unfolds before your very eyes.

Reflections

What did this chapter cause you to reflect upon?

What new hobby or interest have you been wanting to explore?

Identify at least 3 hobbies or interest that you'd like to explore with your partner.

LESSON 15
Love Thyself

Single happy girls know that to love thyself is to know thyself, and I'm solely referring to self-pleasuring. In fact, it is through self-pleasuring that many women first learn about their bodies and what brings them to orgasm. Research shows that children begin self-pleasuring as early as 6-years old, and boys are more likely to masturbate earlier than girls. When girls finally discover the hidden treasure that exists down there; however, the floodgates swing open, and girls become women who start to take ownership and responsibility for their own sexual satisfaction.

Knowing how your body works means just as much to you as it does to any potential mate. Many mature men want to make love to a woman who doesn't have to be taught everything, including what it is that makes her click. No pun intended. This is not to say that they will always do what is needed or necessary to bring you such satisfaction, but great sex begins with you, the woman, knowing what it takes to please you and being able to communicate that to your mate.

Communication is key, but so is comfort with one's own body. You must feel comfortable enough to travel to that deep dark place and get to the heart of your own sexuality. Women who don't feel sexy, valued, or attractive often have a hard time going there to begin with and struggle to reach orgasm. That's why I believe that learning the art of loving one's own body, can be a liberating and empowering act for any woman.

Masturbation is so taboo that the very mention of it sends most people into a panic, yet masturbation is a normal function of life for many. In fact, many men use masturbation to help bring them to orgasm in the first place and vice versa. Ultimately, this is about finding what makes you happy in the bedroom and not being too embarrassed to share it with your mate.

Someone once told me a story about a couple who married young. The woman, as well as the man didn't know much about pleasing the other and so they took their inexperience into the marriage and into their bedroom. The problem was, the woman always got the short end of the stick.

Again, no pun intended. The man on the other hand, as many men do, always reached orgasm, but the woman was left feeling unfulfilled. She had never reached orgasm before marrying him or during the twenty years of their marriage and that was a problem for at least one of them.

There is no doubt in my mind that it would have pleased him to please her, but for some reason or another, he couldn't. However, the question really wasn't about whether or not he could please her, the question was, could she please herself without him. My friend asked her if she had ever masturbated and she told her, no. I thought it strange, that a married couple hadn't tried all there was to experience in the bedroom within reason and respect, because for me as a happy, single girl, there wasn't much I hadn't tried on my own.

These so-called, *experiments* got me through many cold and sometimes lonely nights. These experiments taught me how to give myself pleasure, so that I'd never have to be dissatisfied in a relationship because a man didn't know how or was too selfish to please me in the process of love-making. I didn't want to leave my total satisfaction in the hands of someone else.

If you don't know what pleases you, it's likely that your guy will have a hard time figuring it out as well. It's like trying to give someone directions to a place that you've never been to before. My advice to all single, happy girls and their not so happy friends is to get to know your body and don't be afraid to tell someone *or* show someone how it works.

Men know and understand their bodies and aren't afraid to tell *you* when you're stroking too hard or not quite bobbing right. They'll tell you without hesitation that you're doing it all wrong, and they won't stop telling you until you get it right. Why are we so polite about being dissatisfied in the bedroom? If you know what it takes to make you happy, why not say it *or* if you're too ashamed to say it, then show it. Most men would love nothing more than to watch his woman or wife pleasure herself, and the only thing he has to do is watch, be at attention and ready for duty when called to action. What a wonderful world that could be!

Stop playing nice in the bedroom and stop pretending your needs don't matter. As women, we give so much to others on a daily basis and never ask for much in return, but in the bedroom, it doesn't have to be that way. However, it starts with you first knowing what it is that you want, and if that means taking yourself on a dirty, solo journey to "get you there", then so be it. There's nothing sexy about a woman who's afraid to be dirty in the bedroom. Besides, if you can't be dirty in the bedroom, then where can you be dirty?

Don't get me wrong, sex is not merely an act of pleasing yourself, but rather an act of pleasing your partner. However, your partner can't please you if you don't know what it takes to please you. And if you're too embarrassed, too shy, too resistant, or simply too meek to speak up, then you'll never have a sex life worth caring much about. Your sexual evolution is awaiting you, and my friend, you owe it to yourself to go and find it. If you haven't been down there in a while, it's time you take a visit and discover the gem in your own ocean. You will be glad you did, and hopefully, so will he.

You need to know, though, that *all* men aren't confident enough to embrace a woman exploring sexual satisfaction without him. So, break him in easy. Let him know that you want to have this experience with him because you love him and trust him. Assure him that he turns you on and that you want to take your feelings for him and your sexual life to new heights. Involve him in the process. Let him stroke you down there. Purchase a toy and have him use it on you during foreplay and my last trick of the trade, go out and get a

Brazilian wax. Though I don't believe that most *mature* girls look good without hair down there, the sensation and the arousal that comes from having the hair removed is insatiable! In fact, when I first had it done, my vagina was so sensitive to the touch that a gentle breeze of air brought me immense pleasure!

When it's all said and done, if you're not willing to be the keeper of your own sexual satisfaction and happiness, you can't expect someone else to do it for you. You are the keeper of the "clit". You hold the key to your happiness, and if someone isn't getting you off after you've told him what to do, then you may need to reexamine his commitment to you and your overall relationship. How people show up in the bedroom, is often how they show up in real life. If they aren't giving, nurturing and patient in their day-to-day life, chances are they won't show up that way in the bedroom where all of these attributes really matter.

In conclusion, you can't make someone be something he's not, but you *can* show up for yourself-ready, willing, and able to give *you* what you need, in spite of someone else's failure or unwillingness to do so inside or outside the bedroom.

Reflections

What did this chapter cause you to reflect upon?

What do you like most about your sex life?

What do you like least?

What would make your sex life even better?

LESSON 16
Have It Your Way

I spent my precious 20's "getting to know myself" as so many 20 year-olds do. I believe that if I had gotten married back then it wouldn't have lasted. At the time, I needed counseling to help me work through my childhood trauma, and for many years, I worked through my "stuff" and remained unattached. I also believe that if I had had children back then, I would have probably devoted so much time to loving and caring for them, that what I needed emotionally and mentally could have totally been neglected. So, my 20's passed me by like the Long Island Railroad, yet I didn't mind so much, I still had my 30's.

As for my priceless 30's, I spent those years establishing myself in my career, fixing my credit that I had destroyed in my 20's and dealing with men whom, if I had done the choosing, I probably wouldn't have chosen. Unfortunately, I allowed them to choose me, so my 30's rolled by like a movie on the big screen. I watched but didn't realize that this was *my* life that I was watching, but unlike the movies, I wouldn't have an opportunity to press rewind or pay the fare to see it again. A sinking feeling came over me because never had I wanted something so badly. As I neared the end of the my 30's, I realized that I had almost missed the boat. I had almost allowed myself to reach forty without a husband or child. Though I wanted both, I knew that having a child on my own was far simpler than trying to find a husband and rushing to get married for the sake of a child. To that end, I've decided that I'll have a baby through artificial insemination.

My decision was not easy. I, like many women, wanted my family to come packaged just so, but I now know that everything doesn't come perfectly packaged. Sometimes you must decide that you'll take each item ala carte and build on the rest of the menu. For many single women these days, the child has come before the husband, and while I'm not an advocate of children growing up without fathers in the home, single mothers make it happen against all odds.

The other reality is that sometimes the husband comes first only for a woman to realize that she can't have children *or* maybe he can't. Sometimes, they do have children, but the marriage ends in divorce, and she still ends up being a single mom. Whatever the case may be, a family doesn't always come in the package or the order that society tells us that it should. As single, happy women in the 21st century, we must learn to roll with life and go after what we want, even if it means going against the grain to get it.

When I was in grad school at Northwestern, my colleague Lisa, who was a 50-ish white woman, talked often about her son Nijel who was about 9-years old and her oldest son Michael who was a high school student. She loved her boys, and it showed in everything she said and did. On the outside looking in, she appeared to be a divorced mom of two boys who was just trying to create a better life for her family by obtaining her master's degree in Education. We were all quite shocked to discover that Lisa had never been married AND her youngest son Nijel, was an African-American child. To add to the story, Michael didn't know where or who his father was.

You see, Lisa had decided late in her 30's that she wanted a child. Since she wasn't married or involved in a relationship, she chose artificial insemination. Though the husband never came, she still got her boys *and* much like Burger King, she had it her way. This is not just Lisa's story; there are women raising children as their own that they didn't give birth to, but you would never know unless you asked. Many women have decided to adopt their children or to try for a child on their own through medical procedures that don't require a husband. Whatever the choice is, know that no one but you gets to make it. Waiting for all the gods to line up or for the perfect package to fall on your doorstep could prove disappointing, especially if you're a woman in your late 30's or early 40's and you still want children. The best advice I can give you is don't wait to step into the perfect life, create that life for yourself.

Nothing in life is promised, not a husband or a child, but if you can have a child without compromising who you are as a person, then by all means go for it. When I speak of compromise, I'm talking about those women who marry for the sake of having a child only. They don't love the man. They don't even want the man, but they feel as though he's their only path to motherhood. Frankly, a sperm donor will do. At least with a sperm donor, you don't have to be *married* to this person for a lifetime through this child. If you want the child to know the father, there are banks that have anonymous as well as known donors. If you're really lucky ask someone you know to be a donor, but don't forget to write up a document specifying what the expectations are from both ends. After all, it's business, so treat it as such.

I believe that through technology, women are empowered like never before. If you have the means and are mentally, physically and emotionally fit to take on the responsibility of motherhood, then go for it! It doesn't have to be one of the dreams that you let slip away because a husband never came along. We don't wait on husbands to purchase our first homes or go on our dream vacations, so why risk waiting until it's too late to have a child because we're waiting for a husband to come along?

I have accepted the reality that a husband may not come before I hit 40 or 41 or even 45, but that's not going to stop me from working to have a child on my own. If he happens to come along after the fact, then he can join the clan, but if he comes much later in life, then that's fine too. I know I make it sound so easy, but truly, I understand, this isn't for everyone. It's for those women, like me, crazy enough to take a chance on creating a child out of the pure love I have for myself and the love that I want to share with another human being through motherhood. Honestly, more women than we know get pregnant "by mistake" everyday and the men walk out of their lives, leaving them to raise children as single mothers. Why start a child's life off with all of that drama? If you can save the drama and have the child, why not? It's a new day where women get to be mothers of their own choosing, and I am glad that I woke up just in time to embrace the prospect of motherhood for myself.

Reflection

What did this chapter cause you to reflect upon?

How important or unimportant is it for you to have a child?

Would you consider having a child on your own? Why or why not?

LESSON 17
You're Imperfectly Perfect

I can't tell you how many times I've heard, "You're smart. You're beautiful. So what's the problem?" To which I've shrugged my shoulders and embarked on a failure mission to assist the concerned critic as he/she helped me "figure it out". But if I really knew the answer, do you think I'd still be single? The short answer to their questions is, "nothing's wrong with me". Not every good looking, smart man or woman finds a mate in their 20's or even in their 30's. Many who do often end up divorcing later in life anyway. No one wants to travel down that road.

So, what's wrong with us happy, single girls, and why haven't we locked down *Mr. Right?* Everyone wants to know. Our mothers are concerned. Our grandmothers envy us, because they wish they had waited. Our sisters and brothers feel sorry for us and our coworkers secretly discuss us in the lunchroom. Well, there are a host of reasons that could answer that question, ranging from timing to missed opportunities. There is no science to finding someone amazing to spend the rest of your life with, and if you don't find him, it doesn't mean that there is something "wrong" with you. In fact, there is probably something right with you that prevents you from taking the first man that comes along and living unhappily married for the rest of your life just to say that you have someone.

Society makes single women of a certain age feel as though something's wrong with them. Every tabloid is about how to find a man. They're talking about it in everything from movies to bestselling books, and God forbid you're someone like Halle Berry or Jennifer Aniston. No matter what your mate does to bring about the demise of the relationship, it's your fault, because *you* can't keep a man. When the truth could be, maybe you chose the wrong guy for all the right reasons. Does that really mean something's wrong with you?

I get it, we're not perfect, but to let others make us believe that something is wrong with us because we're still single is not acceptable. We are single for a myriad of reasons and whether it is because we were smart enough to work on the mess from our past before we joined hands in holy matrimony with another poor soul, or it's because we chose careers first and families second, both (and probably many more) are valid and perfectly acceptable. The bottom line is that neither of those choices makes us wrong. They just make us women taking responsibility and control of our own lives instead of being influenced by the standards, opinions, and values of others.

You are imperfectly perfect no matter what anyone has told you, and you're not wrong for choosing to be single. You're not a loser if you can't find a mate. As I mentioned in previous chapters, you may need to look outside your box or get out more often, but to believe that something is *wrong* with you is something I refuse to let you get away with. I won't allow you to make excuses for your shortcomings either, because we all have them! You can't tell me that all of those who are in marriages or long-term relationships are baggage free because I know that just simply isn't true.

People who marry are not better than those who don't, but if we needed to identify a reason, I might conclude that maybe they're more willing to take a chance on love than those of us who are single. I don't know. In fact, I'm pulling from thin air right now, but I'd rather you believe that than to believe that something is wrong with you. You

are the best thing that's ever happened to you and
if it is your wish, perhaps there will be a man who
comes along smart enough to realize it too.

Reflections

What did this chapter cause you to reflect upon?

What do you love most about yourself and what do you hope your future mate will love most about you?

Which lessons in the book were the most beneficial for you and why?

Poetic Expressions of Love

Paradise

Can I see you again
in that dream I've had
for three nights straight
the one I can't seem to shake
where my heart doesn't break
and my soul doesn't ache
or long for your touch

Where it's O.K. to walk alone in the park
and to sleep in the dark

I need to see you
in a place where there are no hesitations
and reservations
are for those who make them
and multiple orgasms
aren't for those who fake them

Can I
see
you
again?

On that hill where I am not afraid to look
down
between the mountains of my heart
where my love can be found
I must
see you
in that place that I've never been
"Where love is a must and lust is no sin
Where God is a woman
and love is within
I need to
see you again?"

Before You

Before you came along
I was so unaware of what was missing
in my life
Going through each day oblivious
That so much ecstasy could exist
From knowing one person
You bring out the best in me
Expect the best from me
And you've made me realize that
only the best
Is meant for me
Before you came along
I was unaware of how much learning
there was to do
You have taught me that the wonders of life
Exist in unspoken words
And that unspoken words
Can travel across many miles
to fill the depth of one's soul
at strange hours of the night
You've taught me to trust myself
And to follow my hearts' desire

No matter where it may lead me
Even if it leads me away from you
You've shown me parts of myself that I
never knew
And parts of myself that had long since
been forgotten
You've helped to unlock mysteries
To dreams that I have shared with no other
Challenged me to be resilient in the face of
adversity
And how to love on levels that only angels
have known
Before you came along
I didn't know what it was like to laugh
everyday
I didn't know what it was like to love a
man in spite of his weaknesses, his faults,
and his beliefs
But today I do
I love you and accept you
for all that you are
And all that you will become
Getting to know the man that smells, feels,
thinks, laughs, and loves the way you do
has been complete gratification
And I look forward to many more
blissful days
To come with you

He is Love

She loved Him more
than caramel
Seducing Hagandaz
On days too hot for soup
More than the love she made
on park benches
in the middle of
Central Park @ 11AM
More than she loved loving those
who didn't love her back
Those who didn't want to embrace
her love
But rather control it
She loved Him more
than she loved the way hungry men
stared @ her ass
and never asked her name
More than her full lips
wrapped around the joy stick of life
Thighs that swayed when she walked
Eyes that took men under and promised
no return

More than she loved gettin' high
to the gospel and mellowing out to jazz
She would do anything for Him
because she loved Him
The way He loved her
Unconditionally
She sang His praises
And humbled herself
As the sun placed itself north of her head
And again as it rested beneath her feet
There was no denying
She'd found love

The Morning After

I woke up this morning.
Lifted my hands from beneath my pillow.
Rubbed my eyes
and opened them,
only to discover that you had gone.
Then I heard your footsteps.
and realized,
you hadn't traveled
too far away.

That Kind of Love

Girl, you got that krazy with a k- kinda love
That can't sleep, got you up all night
kinda love
Got you messin' up on your job, kinda love
A cross between sanity and insane
kinda love

You got that checkin' phones kinda love
Following to see if he made it home
kinda love
Hidin' behind bushes and playin' on
phones kinda love
Don't know if you comin' or goin'
kinda love

You got that could this be love, kinda love
Lovin' him more than yourself kinda love
Scratchin' and keying up cars kinda love
That rockin' in the dark, cause you can't
rest kinda love

You got that, if lovin' you is wrong, I don't

want to be right kinda love
That I'm so in love, I just can't see the light
kinda love
I can't eat, think or breath kinda love
Body aching, heart palpitating, just sick,
kinda love
You got that cryin' while makin' love kinda
love
Dyin' on the inside, cause he won't love
you back kind of love
That, why ain't I good enough for him
kinda love
That I don't think I can live without him
kinda love

You got that, you got it bad kinda love
The one Usher sang about, kinda love
You know, hang up and call right back
kinda love
Yeah, you know what I'm talkin' 'bout,
kinda love

But what you need, is some self, kinda love
Some, I'm beautiful with or without you
kinda love
A little be good to me and I'll be good to
you kinda love
That, stop beating up on yourself girl, kinda
love

You need a little I can love you better, if I
love myself kinda love
I want you, but I don't need the drama
kinda love
That, take me as I am or leave me the hell
alone kinda love
That, never forget who's you are kinda love

Girl, get yourself an ounce of that God in
you kinda love
And stop giving more than you're getting
kinda love
So, you'll always have plenty enough to go
around kinda love
And you'll stop that loving out of fear kinda
love
Girl you deserve only the best there is,
kinda love

In Conclusion

Love has been good to me. I've been blessed to have good men in my life even when I didn't recognize them right away. I have not been abused or mistreated too badly and there isn't a single man that I hold a bad thought about, but I know that this is not the story of many of the women who will read this book.

It is my sincerest prayer that love finds you if that is what you want and when it does, you embrace it for everything it is and everything it is not. We are imperfect souls looking to blend our imperfect existence with one another. Your unions, though they may not be perfect, they will be worth it, if you let go, be open, and be willing to admit to yourself that love is what you make of it.

I am so happy to have completed this work, but now this leads me to the next phase. I am now ready to go and help women across the globe heal from broken hearts, learn to love (again), and become the women that God originally intended them to be. Women are truly a manifestation of God and it is our light that illuminates the world. When we are not happy, the world is not a good place.

I want to teach women how to be happy with or without a partner and to be kinder, gentler critics of their own flaws, for when they do, they will see the men in their lives as mere human beings on a human experience trying to love and be loved just as they are.

In the words of my mentor, friend and coach, Rita Stewart, *We Are Ascending*.

To all of the special people who believed in this project and gave it breath to live. Below are the people who supported my Kickstarter campaign, donated food for my book reading events, and pre-ordered the book just because. In no particular order I extend my gratitude to you.

Christopher Hale

Jamie Lindsey Lawrence

Kellie Sneed

LaTasha Mitchell

Alton Tinker

Dionne Hudson

Mary Goss-Hill

Angela Nirvana

Alice Gatling

Shannon Chambliss

Dennis and Rhonda Chambliss

Rochelle Holmes

Shamia Holmes

Porsha Holmes
Niecy Love
Steve Grossman
Katie Bronson
Diane Russell
Jejuana Brown
Stephanie Grair Ashford
Cruel Valentine
Danielle Morris
Patricia Smith
Deidra Bankston
Jzhanel Cole
Adebayo Adesina
Mary Ann Snyder
Eric Ramsey
Jasper Hagan
Vanessa Bounds
Lisa Larkin
Wanda Crumps
Houston Washington
Byron Jackson
Cindy Rhoden

Kym Gomes
Lanetta Anderson
Maisha Dang-Owolabi
Jeremy Holmes
Stephanie Surratt
Cora Thompson
Aishia White
Cecilia Smith
Sheri Jordan
Lisa Gibson
Rukiya Sims
Mariama Whyte
Malika Ali

To schedule Terré for book signings, book club meetings, and speaking engagements, visit www. terreholmes.com. Also, let Terré know how the book has touched your life or relationships by e-mailing her at terre@terreholmes.com or visiting;

www.facebook.com/lovelessonsbyterre
www.facebook.com/terreholmesspeaks

To order books contact:
Turner Holmes Publishing House, LLC
www.turnerholmespublishing.com

ABOUT THE AUTHOR

Terré Holmes is a social-preneur, mentor, speaker, and writer, living in Chicago, IL. She has turned her life challenges into an empowering message for the masses and her work teaches women and youth how to live lives worth living. She lives and breathes to awaken the brilliance in others.

In her spare time she enjoys cooking, dancing, entertaining family and friends in her home, posting things on Pinterest and traveling and meeting new people at home and abroad. She is the proud aunt of 13 nieces and nephews and the oldest sibling of six. Terré is from Cleveland, Ohio. Having lived in Brooklyn, New York, Abu Dhabi, and now, Chicago, IL, she refers to herself as a resident of the world.